Barefoot Waterskiing

by Walter Oleksy

Consultant:
Jennifer Calleri
Marketing Coordinator
USA Water Ski

CAPSTONE BOOKS

an imprint of Capstone Press
Mankato, Minnesota

Capstone Books are published by Capstone Press
151 Good Counsel Drive, P.O. Box 669, Mankato, Minnesota 56002
http://www.capstone-press.com

Library of Congress Cataloging-in-Publication Data
Oleksy, Walter G., 1930-
    Barefoot waterskiing/by Walter Oleksy.
    p. cm.—(Extreme sports)
    Includes bibliographical references and index.
    Summary: Describes the history, techniques, practice, and competition related to
the sport of barefoot waterskiing.
    ISBN 0-7368-0480-3
    1. Barefoot water skiing—Juvenile literature. [1. Barefoot water skiing.
2. Water skiing.] I. Title. II. Series.

GV840.B37 D54 2000
797.3'5—dc21   99-047922

Editorial Credits
Carrie A. Braulick, editor; Timothy Halldin, cover designer; Kia Bielke, production
    designer; Heidi Schoof, photo researcher

Photo Credits
Gene Lower, 25
Işaac Hernandez/Mercury Press, 11, 17; David Gala, 26-27, 40; Jorge Torres, 38, 43
Rich Pomerantz, cover, 8, 12, 14, 23, 33, 34, 36
Scott Markewitz/FPG International LLC, 18, 28
Transparencies, Inc./Michael Moore, 7, 30
Uniphoto/Kevin Syms, 4; Allan Laidman, 20

Table of Contents

Chapter 1   Barefoot Waterskiing 5

Chapter 2   History 13

Chapter 3   Equipment and Safety 19

Chapter 4   Skills 29

Chapter 5   Competition 37

Features

Photo Diagram 26

Words to Know 44

To Learn More 45

Useful Addresses 46

Internet Sites 47

Index 48

Chapter 1
Barefoot Waterskiing

Barefoot waterskiing is a sport in which people water-ski without skis. Most barefoot water-skiers ski on lakes. Barefoot water-skiers are called "barefooters" or "footers."

Boats tow barefooters across the water. Barefooters hold onto a handle attached to a tow rope. Barefooters ski in the boat's wake. This V-shaped set of waves trails behind a moving boat.

Waterskiing Styles
Most water-skiers use skis to water-ski. They may use two skis. These water-skiers sometimes

Barefooters hold onto handles attached to tow ropes.

perform in ski shows. Water-skiers in ski shows perform various tricks and stunts. They may climb on top of each other to form pyramids. Water-skiers also may use two skis to jump off ramps.

Some water-skiers use only one ski. This is called slalom waterskiing. Slalom skiers often ski through zigzag courses around floatable markers in the water. These markers are called buoys.

Many barefooters perform tricks and stunts without skis. They perform some of these tricks in the air. They may ski backward or on one foot. Some barefooters jump off ramps. They try to jump the longest distance possible. Barefooters often compete against each other in competitions.

One-Foot Skiing and Tumbleturns

Barefooters often ski on one foot. They place their feet about 6 inches (15 centimeters) apart to do this. They transfer almost all of their weight to one foot. Barefooters then put one foot straight out in front of their bodies.

Barefooters turn on the surface of the water to perform tumbleturns.

Barefooters also perform tumbleturns. They spin in a circular motion on the water's surface to perform these tricks. They may perform 180- or 360-degree turns. Barefooters turn halfway around to perform 180-degree tumbleturns. They turn completely around to perform 360-degree tumbleturns.

Front Toeholds and Skiing Backward

Barefooters also perform front toeholds. They use a barefoot toehold harness to perform this trick. This nylon strap fits inside the bridle. A bridle is the two pieces of rope that connect the handle to the tow rope. Barefooters ski on one foot to do a front toehold. They put their free foot deep into the toehold harness. This allows barefooters to ski without having to hold onto the handle.

Some barefooters ski backward. They use a backward barefoot ski to perform this trick. Barefooters begin skiing backward with their back to the boat and both feet on the ski. They hold the handle behind their back. Skiers then take a breath and submerge their head and shoulders under water. They then hold the handle behind their knees. Barefooters slowly rise out of the water as the boat starts to move. They then step off the ski and begin barefoot skiing backward.

Barefooters place one foot in a toehold harness to perform front toeholds.

Jumping

Barefooters sometimes jump off ramps placed in the water. Most of these are made of fiberglass. This strong, light material is made of woven glass fibers. Jump ramps are about 4 to 5 feet (1 to 1.5 meters) wide. They are about 13 feet (4 meters) long and 1.5 feet (.5 meter) high.

Barefooters follow several steps to jump. They start skiing as the boat starts to move. The boat speed reaches about 43 miles (69 kilometers) per hour as they approach the ramp. Barefooters keep their shoulders level as they hit the ramp. They pull the rope toward their chest as they land. Many competitive barefooters can jump nearly 100 feet (30 meters).

Some barefooters jump off ramps.

Chapter 2
History

Waterskiing began in 1922. Ralph Samuelson strapped two large pine boards to his feet. He hung onto a rope as a boat towed him on Lake Pepin, Minnesota.

The First Barefooters
Barefoot waterskiing began in 1947 in Winter Haven, Florida. Slalom skier A. G. Hancock decided to try stepping off his ski. He then began barefoot skiing.

Dick Pope Jr. was the first well-known barefooter. He learned the sport on his own only a few days after Hancock. Newspapers and magazines printed stories about Pope.

Barefooters ski in a boat's wake.

Some barefooters started skiing backward in the early 1960s.

Other people then tried barefoot waterskiing. In 1950, a waterskiing competition in Florida included a barefoot waterskiing event. The barefooter who could barefoot water-ski for the longest time won this event. Barefooters began performing tricks such as tumbleturns and skiing backward in the early 1960s.

Barefoot Waterskiing Gains Popularity

Barefoot waterskiing soon became popular in other parts of the world. It became especially popular in Australia. Australians began barefoot jumping in the late 1960s. In 1978, skiers from 10 countries competed in the first World Barefoot Championships in Canberra, Australia.

Some barefooters formed clubs. In 1961, the first barefoot club in the United States formed. In 1978, the American Barefoot Club (ABC) formed. This organization governs competitive barefoot waterskiing events in the United States. It is part of a national waterskiing organization called USA Water Ski.

Bum Jumping

By 1977, barefoot jumping was popular in the United States. In 1978, jumping was included in the U.S. Barefoot Nationals for the first time.

The United States sent its first barefoot jumping team to the World Barefoot Championships in 1978. William Farrell was on this team. Farrell tried something new at the event. He went up and off the ski ramp while in a seated position. He jumped farther than others who went off the ramp on their feet. People called this jumping style "bum jumping."

Judges later banned bum jumping from competitions. They thought that it was not a true form of barefoot waterskiing. This is because it was not performed on the feet.

Inverted Jumping
In 1989, U.S. barefooter Mike Seipel tried a different style of jumping. He jumped headfirst and let his feet trail behind him while in the air. People called this an inverted jumping style. Most barefooters jumped feetfirst at this time. Seipel broke the world record with his first inverted jump. He jumped 72.5 feet (22 meters). Other barefooters then tried inverted jumping.

Today, barefooters continue to break jumping records by performing inverted jumps. Australian Brett New holds the current world barefoot jump record. He jumped 85.6 feet

Barefoot jumpers continue to perform inverted jumps today.

(26 meters) in 1998. A new video judging system recorded this distance. This system uses a camera to record jumpers' distances. The old system relied on people to record distances. The video system records jump distances more accurately than people can. World jump records recorded without this video system have been disqualified.

Chapter 3
Equipment and Safety

Barefoot waterskiing can be a dangerous sport. Barefooters use equipment to help keep them safe. They make sure this equipment is in good condition. Barefooters also follow safety measures.

Tow Ropes and Handles

Tow ropes for barefoot waterskiing usually are about 75 feet (23 meters) long. They usually are made of non-stretch polyethylene or Kevlar. These strong, waterproof materials stretch very little. This makes rides smooth for barefooters.

Handle sections connect to tow ropes. These sections include a rope handle and

Barefooters' equipment includes a wet suit, tow rope, and handle.

bridle. Handle sections are about 5 feet (1.5 meters) long.

Rope handles are about 1 foot (.5 meter) long. They are made of stainless steel or aluminum. These metals are very strong. Rope handles have grips. These soft, rubber pads make handles more comfortable for skiers to hold.

Barefooters should have plastic-covered bridles and plastic endcaps. Endcaps cover both ends of the handle. These items help prevent skiers from getting rope burns.

Wet Suits and Safety Equipment

Most barefooters wear padded neoprene wet suits. These waterproof rubber suits keep barefooters warm in cold water. They allow a thin layer of water to enter between the skier's skin and the suit. The skier's body heat warms the water. This keeps the skier warm. The padding in wet suits helps protect barefooters from injuries during falls.

Some wet suits are buoyant. These wet suits allow barefooters to float after falls. Barefooters

Barefooters wear wet suits to stay warm in cold water.

must wear buoyant wet suits or life jackets in competitions.

Barefooters wear other safety equipment. Jumpers wear crash helmets to protect their heads from injuries during falls. These helmets have foam padding and a chin strap. Some barefoot jumpers wear a back brace. Barefooters wear these pieces of padded nylon around their waists. Back braces help reduce strain on jumpers' backs during landings. Gloves protect skiers' hands from becoming sore. They also improve a skier's grip on the rope handle. Barefooters make sure their gloves fit tightly around their wrists. This helps prevent barefooters' gloves from sliding down their hands.

Training Equipment

Barefooters often use a barefoot boom to learn to barefoot ski. This metal pole extends about 5 to 10 feet (1.5 to 3 meters) over the side of a boat. Barefooters hang onto booms. They also may attach their handle sections to booms. These skiers then hang onto the handle. Booms keep barefooters in smooth water. This helps skiers keep their balance.

Barefooters often use a boom to practice barefoot waterskiing.

Other barefooters use an extended pylon to learn to barefoot ski. This pole is mounted near the center of a boat. It extends straight up from a boat about 5 feet (1.5 meters). Barefooters attach a tow rope to the extended pylon and hold onto the handle as they ski. Extended pylons give barefooters an upward lift. This helps barefooters stand up on the water. It also can help barefooters learn tumbleturns.

Safety

Barefooters need to follow safety measures. They should be familiar with ski areas. They should make sure the water is free of floating objects. Barefooters who crash into objects may injure themselves. Barefooters also learn how to fall. Barefooters tuck their heads in when they fall. This helps protect barefooters from neck and head injuries. Beginning barefooters learn basic skills before they try to perform tricks.

Safe barefooters communicate with their drivers. For example, they tell their drivers when to speed up, slow down, or stop. They let their drivers know if there is a problem. Barefooters often use hand signals to communicate with their drivers. For example, they put a thumb up when they want the boat's speed to increase. They put a thumb down when they want the boat's speed to decrease.

Barefooters should ski at the proper speed. Barefooters who ski too fast often have dangerous falls. These skiers may injure

Barefooters use hand signals to communicate with their drivers.

themselves. A boat's correct speed for barefoot waterskiing varies. This speed depends on the barefooter's weight. Some barefooters divide their weight by 10 and add 20 to find their correct barefoot waterskiing speed.

Helmet

Wet Suit

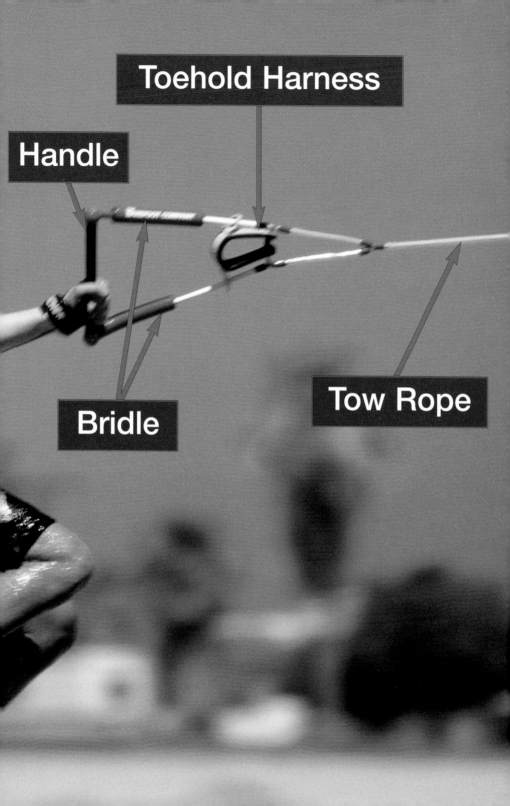

Chapter 4
Skills

Barefooters should have certain skills and abilities. They should be good swimmers. They also should be experienced water-skiers on skis.

Many beginners learn barefoot waterskiing skills at ski schools. Several barefoot waterskiing champions operate schools to teach the sport. Ron Scarpa operates a barefoot waterskiing school in Winter Haven, Florida. Scarpa was the overall world barefoot waterskiing champion in 1998. Mike Seipel operates a barefoot waterskiing school in West Palm Beach, Florida. Seipel has held the world barefoot jump record seven times.

Experienced barefooters can perform tricks.

Body Position

Barefooters should maintain a correct body position as they ski. This helps barefooters keep their balance. They keep their knees bent and their backs straight. They keep their heads up. Barefooters who look down often lose their balance and fall.

Barefooters pay special attention to the position of their feet. Barefooters keep their feet slightly ahead of their shoulders and about one shoulder width apart. Barefooters ski on the soles of their feet. They keep their toes up. Barefooters who catch a toe on the water may fall. Barefooters sometimes keep their toes curled to prevent this. Barefooters let their feet float naturally on the water. Barefooters who dig their heels too far in the water often fall.

Barefooters try to ski on calm water. Barefooters who ski on rough water may be unable to maintain their body position. This may cause them to fall. Barefooters often ski

Barefooters should keep their heads up, backs straight, and knees bent as they ski.

on calm lakes. Rivers and oceans often are too rough for barefooters.

Three-Point Stance
Barefooters should know how to do a three-point stance. Barefooters perform this stance before they do tumbleturns. They sometimes do a three-point stance before they stand up on the water.

Barefooters perform a three-point stance by skiing in a seated position. Their feet are on the water's surface. They keep the handle close to their waist and lean back.

Barefoot Waterskiing Starts
Barefooters move to a standing barefoot skiing position in different ways. Most beginners use a wakeboard to start barefoot waterskiing. These boards look similar to surfboards. They are stable and easy to straddle. Barefooters first sit on the middle of the wakeboard. They put one leg on each side of the board and grab the rope handle. Barefooters lean back and keep their feet above the water as the boat starts to move. They

Barefooters ski in a seated position with their feet on the water to perform a three-point stance.

then push their heels out. They put the soles of their feet on the water. Barefooters then move into a correct barefoot waterskiing position.

Most experienced barefooters know how to perform deep-water starts. These skiers do not use wakeboards or any other equipment to start skiing. Barefooters who do tricks and jumps often perform deep-water starts.

Barefooters who do tricks usually can perform deep-water starts.

Barefooters lay on their backs to perform deep-water starts. They put their feet over the tow rope. They then throw their head back. As the boat starts to move, barefooters apply pressure to the tow rope with their feet. They sit up and move their feet off the tow rope. Barefooters then perform a three-point stance and stand up on their feet.

Steering

Barefooters should know how to steer. This skill is especially important for barefooters who compete in slalom competitions. These barefooters cross back and forth over a boat's wake. Most barefooters who perform slalom even can steer on one foot.

To steer, barefooters bend their knees to move into a lower position than they normally use. They also move their legs closer together. To steer left, barefooters shift their weight to their right foot. To steer right, barefooters shift their weight to their left foot. They turn their knees, hips, and shoulders in the direction of the turn.

Chapter 5
Competition

Barefoot waterskiing competitions are popular throughout the world. Barefooters may compete in national or international competitions. National competitions include competitors who are citizens of one country. National barefoot competitions in North America include the U.S. Nationals and the Canadian Nationals.

International competitions include competitors who are citizens of different countries. International barefoot waterskiing events include the Pan American Games and the World Barefoot Championships. The Pan American Games are held every four years.

Some barefooters perform a variety of tricks in competitions.

Athletes from about 40 countries compete in this event.

The International Water Ski Federation (IWSF) governs the World Barefoot Championships. The IWSF governs waterskiing events around the world. The World Barefoot Championships are held every two years. Barefooters from about 20 countries compete in this event.

X-Games

Barefoot waterskiing was once a part of the X-Games. The ESPN television network hosts the X-Games each year. Athletes from around the world compete in different extreme sports at this competition. The X-Games have made many people aware of barefoot waterskiing.

The X-Games included barefoot jumping events from 1995 to 1998. Peter Fleck won the barefoot jumping event in both 1997 and 1998. In 1998, he jumped 87.5 feet (27 meters).

Barefooters in the X-Games jumped off ramps.

Barefoot jumpers travel at a speed of about 40 miles (64 kilometers) per hour before they go off ramps.

Events

Competitive barefooters compete in three main events. These are slalom, trick, and jump events. Competitors compete in divisions according to their ages. They also compete in either men's or women's divisions.

Slalom barefooters cross back and forth over the boat's wake. They try to cross the wake as many times as they can. Slalom barefooters make two 15-second turns. These turns are called passes. Slalom barefooters usually ski one pass in a forward position and the other pass in a backward position. They may ski on one foot or two feet. They earn one point for each one-foot crossing of the wake. They earn one-half point for each two-foot crossing. The barefooter with the most points at the end of the competition wins.

Barefooters who perform tricks also make two 15-second passes. Judges are in a boat near the barefooters. They award points for tricks. Each type of trick has a specific point value. Judges add points from the two passes. The barefooter with the highest point total wins the event.

Competitive barefoot jumpers travel at a speed of about 40 miles (64 kilometers) per hour. Each barefooter jumps off a ramp three times. Judges record each barefooter's longest jump. The barefooter who jumps the farthest wins the event.

Many competitions have an overall barefoot champion. Judges add up points from slalom, trick, and jump events to determine who wins the overall champion title.

Barefooters sometimes compete in endurance competitions. Barefooters try to stay up longer than other competitors in endurance events.

Most competitive barefooters enjoy challenging themselves. They try to improve their skills. They will continue to test the limits of this extreme sport in the future.

Competitive barefooters continuously seek new challenges.

Words to Know

boom (BOOM)—a pole that extends off the side of a boat; some barefooters use booms to learn how to barefoot water-ski.

extended pylon (ek-STEND-ed PYE-lon)—a pole that extends straight up from a boat; some barefooters attach tow ropes to extended pylons to learn how to barefoot water-ski.

fiberglass (FYE-bur-glass)—a strong, light material made of woven glass fibers; many jump ramps are made of fiberglass.

neoprene (NEE-uh-preen)—a tough, waterproof rubber; many wet suits are made of neoprene.

polyethylene (pol-ee-ETH-uh-leen)—a lightweight, waterproof material used to make some tow ropes

wakeboard (WAYK-bord)—a wide, long board made of fiberglass or aluminum; boats tow people on wakeboards.

wet suit (WET SOOT)—a body suit made of a waterproof material such as neoprene

To Learn More

Favret, Ben. *Complete Guide to Water Skiing.* Champaign, Ill.: Human Kinetics, 1997.

Italia, Bob. *Freestyle Waterskiing.* Action Sports Library. Minneapolis: Abdo & Daughters Publishing, 1993.

Solomon, Mark B. *Waterskiing: Getting Off the Ground!: With 240+ Visual Aids.* Boston: Aquatics Unlimited, 1997.

Walker, Cheryl. *Waterskiing and Kneeboarding.* Action Sports. Mankato, Minn.: Capstone Books, 1992.

Useful Addresses

International Water Ski Federation
C.P. 5537 BO 22
40134 Bologna, Italy

USA Water Ski
American Barefoot Club
799 Overlook Drive
Winter Haven, FL 33884

Water Ski Canada
1600 James Naismith Drive
Gloucester, ON K1B 5N4
Canada

Internet Sites

American Barefoot Club
http://www.barefoot.org

The Barefoot Media Page
http://waterski.pharamond.com/barefooting

International Water Ski Federation
http://www.iwsf.com

1-Stop-Guide—Water Ski Schools
http://www.1-stop-guide.com/water-ski/
    schools.html

USA Water Ski
http://www.usawaterski.org

Water Ski Canada
http://www.waterski.ca

Index

aluminum, 21

back brace, 22
backward barefoot ski, 9
barefoot toehold harness, 9
boom, 22
bridle, 9, 21
buoys, 6

citizens, 37

deep-water starts, 33–34

endcaps, 21
extended pylon, 23

fiberglass, 10
front toehold, 9

gloves, 22

handle, 5, 9, 19, 21, 22–23, 32
hand signals, 24

helmets, 22

Kevlar, 19

lakes, 5, 32

pass, 41
point, 41–42
polyethylene, 19

ramp, 6, 10, 15–16, 41

ski shows, 6
speed, 10, 24–25, 41
stainless steel, 21

tow rope, 5, 9, 19, 23, 34
tumbleturns, 7, 14, 32

wake, 5, 35, 40–41
wakeboard, 32–33
wet suits, 21–22